VIRGO HOROSCOPE 2024

Angeline A. Rubi

Alina A. Rubi

Published Independently

All rights reserved © 2024.

Astrologer: Alina A. Rubi

Editing: Alina. Rubi and Angeline A. Rubi

rubiediciones29@gmail.com

Who is Virgo?

Dates: August 23 - September 22

Day: Wednesday

Color: Brown

Element: Earth

Compatibility: Capricorn, Pisces, Taurus, and Cancer

Symbol:

Mode: Mutable

Polarity: Feminine

Ruling planet: Mercury

House: 6 (health and service)

Metal: Mercury

Quartz: sapphire, carnelian, and amazonite.

Constellation: Virgo

Virgo Personality

Those born under this sun sign are open-minded and usually shy, keeping their cards strategically hidden. It is difficult to unravel what a Virgo is thinking as they are very guarded about what they think.

Virgos are almost always very intelligent and imaginative, spending many hours thinking about subjects that many others would think about only temporarily.

They are usually observant, and patient, sometimes they seem cold, and in fact they find it difficult to make great friends. They are the healer of the zodiac; their heart is pure and innocent. No other sign can make people feel good, they know exactly what to say in every situation.

They know how to value others, care, protect and create a safe environment for their friends to recover at their own pace from losses and sorrows. He is patient, sincere, helpful, and affectionate.

They tend to be discreet, friendly, and fun with other people, and can help solve other people's problems with a skill and good sense that they often lack in their own personal relationships.

They are very generous with time and money, and you can easily see them providing community service or getting involved in charity work. Personally, they are attentive to the needs of those who live with them and the family.

Virgo dislikes dirt, disorder, danger, vague people, and uncertainty. Virgos are extremely practical and intelligent; they can spend a lot of time reflecting on any issue, think of solutions to avoid complex situations or conflicts, and possess a psychic vision that allows them to see and realize many things that other people are unable to perceive.

They are skilled in music, science, and languages. They have an excellent memory, and can be very successful as librarians, clerks, accountants, scientists, social workers, and book publishers.

General Horoscope for Virgo

Virgo this will be a year of great opportunities for you in all areas of your life. Of course, you will also have some challenges that can significantly influence your career and your relationships.

It is advisable that you pursue your goals and maintain balance in everything since you will probably have to postpone some plans. Some setbacks may arise due to your lack of energy, so you should control your emotions and eliminate your negative thoughts.

If you focus you can solve all your problems without any problems and succeed. For this to happen you must eliminate indecision and separate yourself from obsolete views.

At certain times of the year, you will be forced to resort to diplomatic tricks to avoid conflicts with others, specifically in work.

A vacation will be very beneficial for married couples, something to remind them of the initial moments of their relationship. Those who are in a couple should remember to find time for communication.

For singles anything is possible: a short-lived passionate romance with someone you will meet through social networks, a serious relationship with a work colleague, or a romantic outing with someone you will meet at a market.

They will have some family problems, but all will be successfully resolved.

At work you should try to offer your own solutions to problems and accept all additional responsibilities.

Finances will be stable, although in some periods, specifically in the middle of the year, there is the probability of a decrease in your income, or delays in payments. During these stages you should refuse loans and of course do not lend money.

You should listen to the advice of people with more experience than you when making investments.

‘

Your family will sabotage your economy, so you must be very organized with your finances. It is important that you make peace with your loved ones, since in unexpected moments you may need their help.

In general, your health will be good, but you should be careful of infectious diseases and epidemics. Remember to visit your doctor to prevent possible chronic diseases.

You should take great care of the health of your skin and eyes from the harmful effects of the computer and cell phones.

There are months where symptoms of emotional exhaustion or depression may appear and the way to counteract this is to be in nature more often. Also, exercise and meditation will have an excellent effect on your health.

In general, it will be a prosperous year, despite all the changes and unpredictable events. You should refrain from impulsive actions, be patient when living in uncertain situations and above all you should take advantage of favorable circumstances.

It is important to follow your intuition, especially in romantic relationships. Make your decisions, but don't be too hasty either, as you may make a mistake.

Love

In 2024 you can open your heart and bring a new love into your life as you will feel more optimistic about love. This can be a good year for romance, whether you are single or married.

You will receive many lessons of love remember how much you give and receive.

In the middle of the year struggles and problems can become quite evident. It is important to work through problems and have healthy, supportive love in your life. You will have time to smooth things over especially during new Moon periods.

During periods of Mercury retrograde old wounds can get in your way, and it is important to address them.

Your love life and marriage will require constant effort and commitment. With the help of the stars, you will be able to achieve a good balance between emotions and romance. Some Virgos will make important life-altering decisions regarding their love or marriage throughout the year.

Economy

This year you will be able to make progress with your long-term plans, and hard and smart work will pay off. You will gain recognition and connect with important people. This may bring more responsibilities, but you can handle it.

During new Moon periods opportunities may come your way and you will be very successful. You should be enthusiastic about your goals and concentrate on what you want to achieve.

You will have a lot of energy to succeed, as you will be more ambitious and focused. This is truly an excellent year for you to succeed, so start working on your plans and be smart with your choices now so that you don't miss a single opportunity.

Focus on what you are passionate about, gather the information you need and do it in the right way and for the right reasons.

During Full Moon periods you will reach new heights and keep up your pace. You should feel comfortable with how far you have come in such a short time and remember that you deserve it after all the hard work and trials you have endured.

If you don't like the work you are doing, you can make a change. You should try to focus on the work you love, so you can confidently launch into new horizons.

You will receive financial rewards, or new resources that will make your life easier.

Lunar Eclipses can help you solve money problems, finalize financial agreements, and you can let go of your old financial patterns.

If you have traumas with money this would be the time to understand and free yourself from all that energy so you can progress. Money does not make people bad; people make money bad.

Solar eclipses will bring you great financial opportunities, and you will have no problems in terms of money. You will be able to obtain professional success and with this also material abundance.

All your hard work and consistent performance during the last months of 2023 will pay off during 2024. Remember to keep up with technology that will contribute to your growth.

Plan so that you can invest in real estate when your finances are on track. Throughout this year, the planets will be in your favor if you put in the effort.

Virgo try not to be complacent and continue to work hard, investing time and energy so that you have a bright future.

Virgo Health

The year 2024 blesses you with good health and you will have no major worries, however, that does not mean you should be cautious. You will have high energy levels if you follow a good physical regimen, a balanced diet plan and go to your regular medical appointments.

In the middle of the year, you will have some mental health problems due to stress so try to stay optimistic. Try to meditate and exercise, at least try to walk more often. Don't spend your days sitting or lying down watching series on Netflix.

You should pay close attention to the way you nourish yourself nutritionally, as you may be deficient in some vitamins.

Take care of your back muscles, and beware of intoxication with beverages, if you have any problems, you may require hospitalization.

Family

The area of your home and family life in early 2024 will be in turmoil, but it is not likely to last long. There will be problems, but you will know how to solve them quickly.

There is a possibility that you may plan a move, or remodel your home, you will have to take on more family responsibilities. During Full Moon periods you will be able to finalize any changes in the home and resolve problems with the family.

If you want more support from your loved ones, you need to strengthen your relationships with family, or those you consider family, i.e., your close friends.

During periods of Mercury retrograde problems with your family that have not yet been resolved will come to light. You will feel emotionally uncomfortable.

There will be some periods where the health of your family members could be affected, as well as your household finances. During these stages you will have a lot of worries.

Important Dates

2/24- *Full Moon in Virgo*. *This is generally a time of intense emotions, and you can see the results of what you have done so far. You can be sensitive and more focused on yourself. Try to give yourself a break.*

7/25- Mercury enters Virgo

8/ 5- *Venus enters Virgo*.

 8/ 5- *Mercury begins retrograding in Virgo*. *Try to be gentle with yourself, don't demand perfection from yourself and plan before the retrograde arrives to tackle the little things so you don't worry about them during the retrograde. This can be great for second chances, so focus on that.*

08/22- *The Sun enters Virgo*.

 9/ 03- *New Moon in Virgo*. *This is usually a good time for energy, enthusiasm, and opportunities. There may be new opportunities that excite you and you can focus on what you want to do for yourself. You can take the initiative with what you want, and you can make things happen.*

 09/18- *Partial Lunar Eclipse in Pisces your opposite sign*

Virgo Monthly Horoscopes 2024

January 2024

This month is not conducive to change and making important decisions, but if your intuition tells you it will work, act on your hunches.

Life as a couple will be very difficult. There is a tendency for arguments and disagreements. These conflicts can also happen in other close relationships, such as your best friends.

You can lose patience easily and become very demanding and jealous. During this month, you will have a lot of problems that have been accumulating and it will be the time to resolve them.

You must make the necessary adjustments because you will function better accompanied to move your projects forward.

You will be involved in legal processes that will not be favorable to you because there will be confrontations with declared enemies. Try to behave diplomatically so as not to aggravate such conflicts.

You will be exposed to defamation, scandal, or envy, and you will find it difficult to maintain your current position. You will not be satisfied with your luck, but it is important that you keep your mind positive in the face of any challenge. The mistakes of your past will be the main cause of these inconveniences. You must face them and repair them as much as possible.

Fantasies will disturb your love life. If you are married or engaged, your partner will be your grounding wire. If you have no one, don't be tormented by fantasies and illusions that pop up every time you meet someone as you will be very romantic and affectionate.

It is likely that conflicts will arise in your home and that they will disturb your peace of mind. Try not to get involved in problems emotionally, use your reasoning to better analyze your reactions. Some alterations in your health are also probable due to the lack of emotional balance. Take care of your nerves and your diet.

Lucky numbers
4 - 9 - 11 - 14 - 35

February 2024

This month you can face very powerful enemies that will cause difficulties or obstacles in achieving your goals. You may also experience impulsive behaviors that will be unfavorable to you.

It will be difficult for you to exercise self-control, but it is healthy to try. You must analyze the conditions of your past that may still be influencing you and free yourself. This will require a process and conscious work.

Legal problems should be approached with care to avoid complications or deception.

You will be able to make good business deals and sign contracts, but you will have to be smart to do so.

At the end of the month, you will be more aggressive than at other times. It is convenient that you do not repress these energies and that you seek to channel them in a creative way. You should be careful of toxic substances that can contaminate your body.

It is recommended that you emphasize your diet, look for a diet that provides you with vitamins, minerals, and healthy nutrients.

It is important that you take care of your energy levels and do not overload yourself with work or obligations.

Illnesses that may appear will reflect your physical neglect and may also have psychosomatic origins.

During this month, you will begin a diet that will benefit you enormously.

Lucky numbers
3 - 10 - 12 - 26 - 35

March 2024

You'll be eager to make amends for the mistake you made and won't know where to start. However, it's simple: apologize.

Don't hesitate to show yourself as the fun person you are, if you don't have a partner, because whoever you are interested in is waiting for a new spark in their life.

You must learn to prioritize your expenses, because, although you are a good creditor, you leave many empty spaces in your obligations, and in addition to suffering delays and hardships, you end up paying surcharges. Make a list of your payments and put your biggest debts first.

The offers you are given may be misleading, since they suppose a saving that in reality is not true. It is better that you let this opportunity pass you by, as it will only be an expense that you cannot afford and that will hurt your budget. Better opportunities will come.

Try to eat better, hydrate yourself, do an exercise routine and respect your rest hours. Don't go back to a place you were happy hoping to recapture the past, it is already inhabited by other people.

Lucky numbers
2 - 4 - 9 - 14 - 31

April 2024

You will earn a lot of money during this month as your monetary possibilities will expand. Business will give you the expected result and sometimes a little more. The feeling of growing and being powerful financially will be very strong, but in its negative aspect it could lead you to spend more than you should.

You will have to be moderate with your purchases or expenses because you could incur debts without noticing it. You will wish not to deprive yourself of anything and it is likely that you will not be able to distinguish between what you really need and what you do not.

In any case, you will not lack money and it would be very profitable for you to invest it in your real goals. It is important that you be consistent and not disperse your resources in goods that only serve to please your status or highlight your social position.

You must learn to value the benefits your partner adds to your life. You don't value the way he or she has positively influenced your life. That is called ingratitude.

You must learn to adapt to the conditions imposed on you, it is not intelligent to face an order of things that you do not control.

You will find that at the end of the month things could be a bit difficult and unruly on their own, but if you connect correctly with others, the most difficult tasks will be done almost effortlessly. If you ask someone for a favor, that person won't want to help you, although everything can be different if you approach tactfully. Start with a compliment, then ask for the favor and you will see how you get what you ask for.

You should not give yourself the luxury of being paralyzed, it is time to move forward and give a solution to any problem you have. You are stagnating your progress to give way to a period of stagnation that could last a long time if you do not put the brakes on it right now, it sounds sarcastic to say that you should stop something that is stagnant, but that's just the way it is.

Lucky numbers
2 - 3 - 13 - 19 - 25

May 2024

Having faith is good, but it does not make you money. You must give up those reports of good intentions and ask for concrete facts. It is time for actions and not empty promises. Actions are what count. If you continue with this passivity you will continue to lose resources. It is time to get down to work and not sit and wait.

The boredom you feel is due to a lack of goals. To avoid this emotion, and to get your life moving, you must set yourself new challenges. The most important of all must be the care of your mind and soul. That is the feat on which you must concentrate.

A spectacular moment will happen with the person you love this month. Don't allow people who don't know you to be so intrusive in the decisions you have made regarding a sentimental issue that has been on your mind.

The environment in which you surround yourself is not willing to stand by your side, nor is it willing to support you in a matter that you cannot handle on your own, you are likely to see your options on an important matter reduced.

If you are single in your love life, there will be complications if you don't start listening more to your desires. It is very likely that you don't realize that this person has crept into your heart very quickly and you are not giving him or her the attention he or she deserves.

Lucky numbers
3 - 9 - 22 - 26 - 30

June 2024

Your health will depend a lot this month on how much you cleanse your environment and yourself this month. Do detoxification treatments, drink teas, and eat foods that don't put pressure on your body, and exercise. When you break up with friends who poison you with their toxic attitude, you will feel better. Do it with determination.

There will be a drastic change in your bank account, you must be careful when spending and investing. Analyze your expenses and check their validity.

To be happy with your partner, you cannot rush anything, let the relationship walk at its own pace. This is the month to show your sensuality to the world, to assert yourself, to ask for what you want. You need fresh air: do not postpone your date with happiness.

Relax, and if you feel out of shape help yourself with home methods to combat lack of energy.

Your projects and ideas will continue to move forward, but instead of rushing things, take the opportunity to refine your ideas.

You must make important decisions in your life that will lead you to take the right steps and get what you want and have dreamed of.

Don't be remembering the past, that is not healthy as it stops your progress in life and makes you less attentive to what you need to do to succeed.

Some people will come to tell you that you are doing something wrong in your life, but you should only pay attention to them if they are people you trust.

 Don't let the opportunity to meet someone very special slip away at the end of the month, you may need to pay extra attention to that person to get to know them better.

Lucky numbers
5 - 27 - 32 - 33 - 34

July 2024

It is not advisable to always be looking backwards, the present is more wonderful, it just may present challenges that are more difficult to achieve.

You are afraid that your partner will find out about something related to your past. You think that if she finds out, her image of you will change for the worse. She already knows and understands you. It is not necessary for you to hide.

To attract the necessary good energies in your love you must make a ritual during the stage of Full Moon.

Bad economic decisions should not be repeated. You have learned the hard way, and you must honor that learning. You have more wisdom about the art of making money because of these experiences.

Apathy should not take control of your life. Keep up your enthusiasm, for you may fail in other aspects of your life, but a Virgo never makes mistakes when it comes to taking care of his or her body.

At the end of the month, you should not make a risky decision about your finances, always remember to have clear goals regarding money.

Lucky numbers

7 - 10 - 11 - 18 - 30

August 2024

This month do not let a moment of separation with your partner make you throw away everything you have lived together. Nothing lasts forever, only love. It may not last forever, but you must live strive to make it so. All problems must be solved immediately, all lies and deceptions must be discussed and forgiven.

If you are looking for a partner it is not always good to have the patience of the world with that person who has bewitched you, remember that you will not always give this benefit to all the people you meet.

You must avoid repeating the mistakes of your past, so use new techniques. Behave as if you are doing everything you are doing for the first time. This attitude will allow you to find new ways of doing things.

You should not put the care of your mind and state of mind on people who see this task as an ordinary job. In addition to that help, put away from your mind all negative thoughts that harm you. Don't let anyone speak for you, raise your voice when your rights are at stake.

Lucky numbers
14 - 16 - 24 - 25 - 27

September 2024

It is a good month to choose a day and sit down with your partner, with a glass of wine or other liquor, and talk about how far you have come. Acknowledge the road you've traveled, all the problems you've solved and all the good you've done for each other.

If you are looking for a partner, perhaps, you are wondering what kind of entertainment that person participates in because you do not dare to propose any. You should go slowly and go for the conventional: a simple trip to the movies or the theater.

You should not underestimate the price of the talent of your partners in work or business, because after all you are part of a structure, and what you restrict, can be limited to you. Remember that in all areas of life the laws of karma are fulfilled: Give what you wish to receive.

Your spirit of persuasion will be your forte, specifically at work, don't overdo it, it can have a negative impact on your work relationships. You will get along very well with your friends, but your need to feel free will be stronger, so give yourself space and use it for relaxation.

Lucky numbers
6 - 10 - 12 - 19 - 25

October 2024

This month you should focus on large projects, as this will be beneficial for you. A business trip will have a positive effect on your professional image. Professional opportunities will arise. It is a good idea to think twice before making important decisions in the financial area.

Every head is a world unto itself, so you should respect your partner's boundaries. You will never know what your partner is thinking, and that is normal. You can't spend 24 hours a day worrying because his mind is elsewhere, far away from you. He has his worries, and you are not the only thing that exists in his world.

If you have not yet found a partner and you are interested in a person, all that gossip about the person you are interested in should be ignored. Remember that no one is perfect, and everyone has a past.

You could benefit from a little rest. Don't exhaust yourself with other people's burdens, plan a weekend cruise, or dedicate a weekend to activities that inspire you. It would also be helpful to visit a museum or theater.

You will have an opportunity to be promoted at a professional level, this opportunity should not be missed.

Lucky numbers
3 - 7 - 10 - 22 - 29

November 2024

This month you will have more time to spend with your loved ones, remember that relationships always require serious work; family should never be put on the back burner.

The desire to prove your superiority can become a serious problem.

There are those who do not agree with your opinions, and that will bring conflict. To give vent to that kind of energies try to be creative.

The financial situation will be stable, and you will earn extra money. You are likely to receive a salary increase or a bonus now that the end of the year is approaching.

You will have some expenses that will undermine your budget, it is better that you plan your purchases together with your loved ones so you can share expenses especially if you are planning a vacation for the end of the year.

At the end of the month, misunderstandings between couples will intensify. you will have to choose between your profession or your family.

In any case, your financial situation will begin to improve, and you will be able to reach a high level of income.

Lucky numbers
16 - 18 - 22 - 26 - 33

December 2024

Singles this month will live moments of happiness. Morpheus or destiny will knock on your doors, you just need to take the first step. There are good planetary aspects that show that this approach to the person you are interested in will be effective.

This will be a month where you will see your efforts rewarded as you will be offered a partnership that will propel your life to places you had not imagined.

You must be prepared for a period that will demand a monumental level of effort from you. You need to find mental and physical balance, i.e., be in harmony. Consider enrolling in yoga or meditation sessions to protect your body and mind.

If you have a partner, remember that the past cannot be changed. You've been prying into your partner's life before you started the relationship, and that complicates things. You must live in the here and now. You are allowing these problems to take center stage and that is creating anxiety and insecurities.

If this month you need to splurge on some deserved luxury or year-end gifts, go for it. Life is meant to be enjoyed and sometimes it's nice to treat yourself.

This month a fortunate event can make you earn more money or start a business that will make you a lot of money. Remember that it is one thing to spend and another to waste.

It is possible that you decide to make some physical change, or you are in the process of cosmetic surgery, that will give you strength and will raise your self-esteem. If you still doubt it, you should make the decision because it will be very good for you.

Important changes are beginning to take shape in your profession. If you are working, you will receive recognition and that will make you feel validated.

You will receive extra earnings, and this will motivate you to make investments, take risks as far as possible. It is drawn in the stars that you will receive very good news related to your future and that will cheer you up at the end of the year. Do you realize it? When your self-esteem is healthy and your energy vibrates high, everything concludes as you want and deserve.

Lucky numbers
12 - 26 - 31 - 33 - 34

The Tarot Cards, an Enigmatic and Psychological World.

The word Tarot means "royal road", it is a millenary practice, it is not known exactly who invented card games in general, nor the Tarot in particular; there are the most dissimilar hypotheses in this sense.

Some say that it arose in Atlantis or Egypt, but others believe that tarots came from China or India, from the ancient land of the gypsies, or that they arrived in Europe through the Cathars. The fact is that tarot cards distill astrological, alchemical, esoteric, and religious symbolism, both Christian and pagan.

Until recently, if you mentioned the word 'tarot' to some people, it was common for them to imagine a gypsy sitting in front of a crystal ball in a room surrounded by mysticism, or to think of black magic or witchcraft, but nowadays this has changed.

This ancient technique has been adapting to the new times, it has joined technology and many young people feel a deep interest in it.

Young people have isolated themselves from religion because they believe that they will not find the solution to what they need there, they realized the duality of this, something that does not happen with spirituality. All over the social networks you find accounts dedicated to the study and tarot readings, since everything related to esotericism is fashionable, in fact, some hierarchical decisions are made considering the tarot or astrology.

What is remarkable is that the predictions that are usually related to tarot are not the most sought after, the ones related to self-knowledge and spiritual counseling are the most requested.

The tarot is an oracle, through its drawings and colors, we stimulate our psychic sphere, the innermost part that goes beyond the natural. Many people turn to the tarot as a spiritual or psychological guide because we live in uncertain times, and this pushes us to seek answers in spirituality.

It is such a powerful tool that tells you concretely what is going on in your subconscious so that you can perceive it through the lens of a new wisdom.

Carl Gustav Jung, the famed psychologist, used the symbols of tarot cards in his psychological studies.

He created the theory of archetypes, where he discovered an extensive sum of images that help in analytical psychology.

The use of drawings and symbols to appeal to a deeper understanding is frequently used in psychoanalysis. These allegories are part of us, corresponding to symbols of our subconscious and our mind.

Our unconscious has dark areas, and when we use visual techniques, we can reach different parts of it and reveal elements of our personality that we do not know. When you can decode these messages through the pictorial language of tarot, you can choose what decisions to make in life to create the destiny you really want.

The tarot with its symbols teaches us that a different universe exists, especially nowadays where everything is so chaotic, and a logical explanation is sought for everything.

The Star, Tarot Card for Virgo 2024

It symbolizes positive thinking, good humor, and good physical health.

Meditation is symbolized by this card. It indicates that you will be able to find new talents and achieve your goals if you are creative.

It is a year of rest and renewal.

Hope, healing, faith, good health, desires that will be fulfilled, optimism, spiritual enlightenment, and integration of the divine with the earthly.

Light in the darkness. Everything becomes clear and all evil dissolves.

It announces that everything where you have concentrated your hopes will be realized, your sincere aspirations, your authentic desires, all will come true.

It announces beneficial encounters in the economic area, it may be an unexpected arrival of money. Because of a loan, a small inheritance, a gift, etc.

For singles, it predicts love. It suggests that conflicts, health problems, and debts will end. Separations become reunions.

In short, it indicates peace, prosperity, and harmony. It signals the help of someone who will act as your protector.

Runes of the Year 2024

Runes are a set of symbols that form an alphabet. "Rune" means secret and symbolizes the noise of one stone colliding with another. Runes are an ancient visionary and magical method.

Runes do not serve for exact predictions, but they do serve to guide you about a future event, a subject, or a decision.

The runes have a specific meaning for the person who wants it, but also some message related to the adversities that arise in life.

Inguz, Rune of Virgo 2024

Inguz's advice is to finish what you start to achieve new goals. This Rune gives you the intuition to know when to start, or when to finish. It can also indicate fertility and prosperity.

This year you must start a new lifestyle, leaving the old behind. Forget the past and the things that hindered your path, flow with the universe.

It is important that you move away from the toxic influences of certain people around you. Any month is good to initiate a change, but this rune advises you to have the best attitude during this year of spiritual rebirth.

If you are single, you should be very cautious and take care of your heart, so you don't get hurt. Don't be fooled by a relationship that seems like a fairy tale. If you have a partner or are married, it portends that it is the perfect time to think about having children. This rune has the nature of helping to conceive, whoever needs it.

He advises you to reflect on what is important for your life, since the way your business will be profitable depends on it.

With determination, you will be able to make your dreams come true, which will bring great financial benefits to you.

Lucky Colors

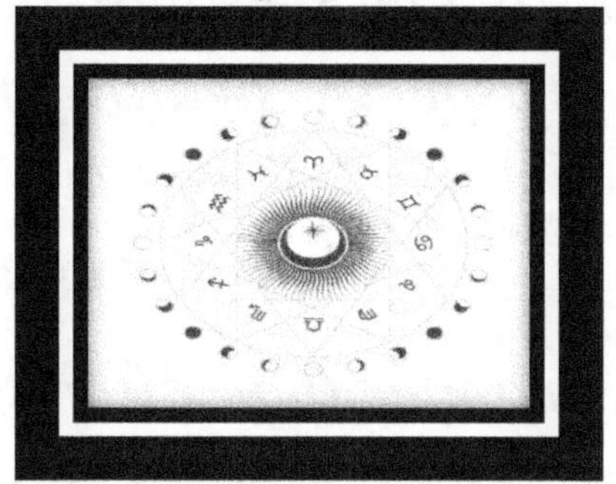

Colors affect us psychologically; they influence our appreciation of things, opinion about something or someone, and can be used to influence our decisions.

Traditions to welcome the new year vary from country to country, and on the night of December 31 we take stock of all the positive and negative things we experienced in the year that is leaving. We start thinking about what to do to transform our luck in the new year ahead.

There are several ways to attract positive energies towards us when we receive the new year, and one of them is to wear or wear accessories of a specific color that attracts what we wish for the year to begin.

Colors have energetic charges that influence our lives, so it is always advisable to receive the year dressed in a color that attracts the energies of what we want to achieve.

For that there are colors that vibrate positively with each zodiac sign, so the recommendation is that you wear the clothes with the hue that will make you attract prosperity, health, and love in 2024. (These colors can also be used during the rest of the year for important occasions, or to enhance your days).

Remember that, although it is most common to wear red underwear for passion, pink for love and yellow or gold for abundance, it is never too much to include in our attire the color that is most important for us.

Virgo

Gray.

Gray key words*: permanence, greatness, great organizational skills, humanitarian skills, isolation, freedom.*

The color gray is related to self-sufficiency and self-control because it is a color that acts as a shield against external influences and can link the material world with the spiritual. Gray is a neutral color and is considered to represent wisdom.

It helps us to reach a state of harmony between two extremes, so that we can see things from a much broader perspective. This benefits us as we can better understand reality and see life from a more unbiased perspective.

Gray also helps us to persevere and be neutral during difficult events, so that we can make decisions without being influenced by our emotions.

This color will help you connect with your true essence, and you will be able to see life from a broader approach. You will be able to find the balance between your desires and needs, and thanks to that you will make wise decisions and live a full life.

It is a very elegant tone that you can combine not only in your clothes but also in the design of your home combined with other colors.

Lucky Charms

Who doesn't own a lucky ring, a chain that never comes off, or an object that they wouldn't give away for anything in the world? We all attribute a special power to certain items that belong to us and that special character that they assume for us makes them magical objects.

For a talisman to act and influence circumstances, its bearer must have faith in it, and this will transform it into a prodigious object, able to accomplish everything that is asked of it.

Usually, an amulet is any object that propitiates good as a preventive measure against evil, harm, disease, and witchcraft.

Amulets for good luck can help you to have a year 2024 full of blessings in your home, work, with your family, attract money and health. For the amulets *to work properly you should not lend them to anyone else, and you should always have them at hand.*

Amulets have existed in all cultures and are made from elements of nature that serve as catalysts of energies that help create human desires.

The amulet is assigned the power to ward off evils, spells, diseases, disasters or to counteract evil wishes cast through the eyes of others.

Virgo Amulet

Celtic Cross.

The Celtic Cross symbolizes the desire to discover and experience the mysteries of life and is a compass that will guide you through your spiritual journey.

It reflects the hope that the Celts had, and one of the Celtic pieces with more symbolism and power in magic. It represents knowledge, strength, compassion, and infinite love.

The mystical, the divine and the sacred harmonize in this symbol, used in many civilizations as an amulet. It is a powerful good luck charm. It is protective, and if you wear it you will have peace, harmony, balance, and wisdom.

Lucky Quartz

We are all attracted to diamonds, rubies, emeralds and sapphires, obviously precious stones. Semi-precious stones such as carnelian, tiger's eye, white quartz, and lapis lazuli are also highly prized as they have been used as ornaments and symbols of power for thousands of years.

What many do not know is that they were valued for more than their beauty: each had a sacred significance, and their healing properties were as important as their ornamental value.

Crystals still have the same properties in our days, most people are familiar with the most popular ones such as amethyst, malachite and obsidian, but nowadays there are new crystals such as larimar, petalite and phenacite that have become known.

A crystal is a solid body with a geometrically regular shape, crystals were formed when the earth was created and have continued to metamorphose as the planet has changed, crystals are the DNA of the earth, they are miniature stores that contain the development of our planet over millions of years.

Some have been bent to extraordinary pressures and others grew in chambers buried deep underground, others dripped into being. Whatever form they take, their crystalline structure can absorb, conserve, focus and emit energy.

At the heart of the crystal is the atom, its electrons, and protons. The atom is dynamic and is composed of a series of particles that rotate around the center in constant motion, so that, although the crystal may seem motionless, it is a living molecular mass that vibrates at a certain frequency, and this is what gives energy to the crystal.

The gems used to be a royal and priestly prerogative, the priests of Judaism wore a plate on the chest filled with precious stones which was much more than an emblem to designate their function, as it transferred power to the wearer.

Men have worn stones since the stone age as they had a protective function guarding their wearers from various evils. Today's crystals have the same power, and we can select our jewelry not only according to their external attractiveness, having them near us can boost our energy (orange carnelian), clean the space around us (amber) or attract wealth (citrine).

Certain crystals such as smoky quartz and black tourmaline can absorb negativity, emitting a pure and clean energy.

Wearing a black tourmaline around the neck protects from electromagnetic emanations including that of cell phones, a citrine will not only attract wealth, but will also help you keep it, place it in the wealthy part of your home (the back left most away from the front door).

If you are looking for love, crystals can help you, place a rose quartz in the relationship corner of your house (the back right corner furthest away from the front door) its effect is so powerful that you may want to add an amethyst to offset the attraction.

You can also use rhodochrosite, love will come your way.

Crystals can heal and give balance, some crystals contain minerals known for their therapeutic properties, malachite has a high concentration of copper, wearing a malachite bracelet allows the body to absorb minimal amounts of copper.

Lapis lazuli relieves migraine, but if the headache is caused by stress, amethyst, amber or turquoise placed above the eyebrows will relieve it.

Quartz and minerals are jewels of mother earth, give yourself the opportunity, and connect with the magic they give off.

Lucky Quartz Virgo 2024

Jade

It functions as a protective energy in the place where it is found. It is associated with stability and security. This quartz is beneficial to have it in a specific place because when we carry it with us it can cause discord with our friends or colleagues.

It helps you to think positive, symbolizes peace, and introspection. This quartz will give you all the strength you need to move forward. It is a stone that will help you to release all the emotions that block you, and to see life with positive lenses. It helps with the proper functioning of the kidneys, heart, and stomach.

There are several colors of jade: blue and green jade, signifying peace, and reflection. Brown jade, related to the earth element, and productivity. Green jade, accelerates the nervous system, moving us to a state of peace in which we can eliminate any negative feelings we feel. Orange jade helps in emotional management, red jade, used to channel tensions and solve problems in harmony. White Jade is the perfect help to make decisions and to know which direction is the perfect one. Yellow Jade brings us joy and helps us to relate to others.

Compatibility of Virgo and the Zodiac Signs

Virgo is an earth sign represented by the goddess of agriculture. Virgo is skilled and methodical, thorough, and seeks to improve herself, making her one of the best partners in the zodiac. Virgo is a scholar, and inspiring words and ideas are aphrodisiacs for this earth sign.

Virgo tends to be a voracious reader, movie buff or music lover. As a mutable sign, they are also open-minded, an attribute that often manifests itself in their exquisite tastes.

Virgo appreciates art that falls into many categories and loves to be aware of new authors. Virgo relies on logic and organization when it comes to matters of the heart, and this whimsical sign is looking for a partner who fits in with their day-to-day.

Virgo uses a database to create a complete representation of their partner, all the people in their life, and their habits, are accumulated in a mental record, with their habits, and dislikes.

Virgo loves to help through their support and practicality, and this earth sign always perseveres to offer viable solutions to conflicts.

Virgo's desire for excellence can take its toll on those around them, and their analysis goes from thoughtful and subtle to overly critical. To maintain healthy relationships, Virgo should not be judgmental and should allow loved ones to walk in their shoes.

Something very important for Virgo to keep in mind is that the continuous search for perfection can become destructive.

When it comes to sexuality, this sign has a lush energy, but is naive. Ruled by Mercury, their sexuality is of an inquiring nature; they look at almost every aspect of sex, including their partner's physique.

There is always beauty in the flaw, so it is important for Virgo to recognize that what amounts to a flaw can be a utility, rather than a defect.

This intellectual sign gets very turned on by humor and intelligent conversation. In theory, Virgo would make an amazing romance novelist, but if your Virgo lover isn't Nicholas Sparks or Corin Tellado, he or she is likely to show it in an abbreviated way. Don't be surprised if your Virgo lover is quite withdrawn in the bedroom, at least at first.

Virgo is a person of routines, until he manages to develop a dialogue, he will be a loving spectator who will be very attentive to what happens in bed.

That doesn't mean he's not depraved, in fact, Virgo loves to be passionate in the bedroom, in a safe environment, Virgo will want to engage in regular sex that allows him to plumb all your inclinations. But don't try something out of the blue, sudden changes in movement or roles will disorient him.

Virgo loves to be helpful and use their skills whenever they can, so they are prone to being a sponge for other people's problems. The best way to combat this is to keep things simple.

Although your Virgo partner is passionate, don't make him or her the watchdog of all your setbacks. If you dump all your stress on Virgo, he or she will feel overwhelmed. Consider looking to your friends for your frustrations.

To have a lasting relationship with Virgo, it is important that you know he will be reliable, but he will also need to count on you especially when he is wrong.

Don't criticize Virgo, it may seem ironic, but Virgo hates to be called attention to his behavior. This will empower him to come to you for help, strengthening the relationship.

As Virgo strives for an impossible ideal in love, when the utopia of perfection dissipates, Virgo will completely give up on the relationship, without informing his or her partner.

He does not intend to be indecent; he strictly hates to disappoint people and, therefore, will want to leave the relationship without having a difficult discussion. In other words, Virgo likes to disappear without leaving a trace.

If you manage to get in touch with your Virgo partner before she reaches for other arms, she will make excuses for herself, and try to defuse the tension by taking on the whole burden. When a breakup happens surprisingly, she has a hard time letting go, will mentally replay every detail of the relationship repeatedly to discover the key moment when things took a 180-degree turn.

Virgo is not always black and white, in fact, he is a very complex creature and if he finds enough information to conclude that his current relationship is flawed, he is willing to look elsewhere for a satisfactory relationship.

__Virgo and Aries__ is a valuable relationship. Aries loves to make promises, but sometimes does not keep them. In this couple the analytical Virgo will be sure not to credit Aries' ostentations. Aries, on the other hand, will be surprised by Virgo's insecurity.

Within this relationship, Aries will be held accountable for his moves, this may result in Virgo's ego becoming inflated when he detects fractures in Aries' methods.

Virgo and Aries must admit Aries' sporadic miscommunication, and Aries' tantrums. If Virgo can work on learning to tolerate Aries' blindness, and Aries can work on releasing his pride, this partnership can be solid.

Virgo and Taurus*, if they agree, a relationship is possible. Ruled by Mercury, Virgo is always processing details of the many pieces of information it gathers daily and chooses to express itself through organized communication.*

This pragmatic sign feels very acclimated when paired with the sensual and material Taurus, who values Virgo's methodical eye and attention to detail.

There are some specific differences between these two signs. Taurus' sensual tendencies can annoy Virgo, which in turn can cause Taurus to feel unbalanced. Favorably, these two signs can overcome obstacles.

Virgo and Gemini*, although the pair may seem incongruous at first, the withdrawn Virgo and the communicative Gemini have much in common. Both Virgo and Gemini are ruled by Mercury, the planet of* *communication, so these two signs are deeply involved with the art of information.*

Gemini loves to collaborate, and the shrewd Virgo is a subtle observer who loves to process information. Although Gemini's characteristic gallantry annoys Virgo a bit, their romantic anxieties can easily be lessened by honest and direct dialogue. If Gemini respects Virgo's needs this relationship can be excellent.

Virgo and Cancer, *it can be a mutually supportive relationship. Particularly, both Virgo and Cancer tend to speculate too much.*

Virgo is preoccupied with trifles, turning every context into the worst possible environment. Similarly, Cancer pays consideration to impalpable shifts in energy, noticing even the tiniest change in body language or verbal tone.

Virgo and Cancer sometimes feed their own anxieties, causing even more fear and mania. However, because they process stress differently, this relationship offers the opportunity for healing. Because they are reflective and advocates for each other, when they pair up, they nurture each other.

Virgo and Leo *is a rewarding relationship. Virgo upsets Leo, this fire sign does not conceive why Virgo is so risk averse. Virgo, on the other hand, knows that life is much more complex than being distracted, everything takes time, and patience. Because of this discrepancy, it is not always easy to navigate a Virgo and Leo relationship. However, if each sign approaches the relationship with an open mind, they can form an inspiring love.*

Virgo and Virgo*, it is an exciting relationship. One of the most significant peculiarities of Virgo is their self-demanding nature. Virgo loves to help, in a tangible way, however, when paired with another Virgo, this quality gets a little twisted.*

In a romantic relationship, two Virgos will try to fix each other tirelessly, each driven by the idea that their methodology is superior. Virgo hates conflict, and this tension can become increasingly aggressive, which will result in many spiteful comments.

The relationship of two Virgos is not doomed, if they manage to explore their individual strengths, they can help each other in different situations. If they guide each other with love, instead of criticizing each other, they can build an affectionate relationship.

Virgo and Libra *have different criteria about perfection, and both are super idealistic. Virgo wants life to be systematized, and Libra seeks harmony. When they come together, they can merge their individual skills, building a relationship that is the epitome of camaraderie. However, while both Virgo and Libra desire a relationship of integrity, they must learn to accept that no relationship is without flaws.*

In fact, healthy conflict can help promote a relationship, i.e., friction can move the relationship forward. By accepting your faults, you can build a sustainable union.

Virgo and Scorpio *make an excellent couple. There is no zodiac sign more related to sex than Scorpio, and this water sign is known for its erotic electricity. Virgo, on the other hand, has the opposite reputation because its symbol alludes to a mythological archetype, often perceived as flawless.*

Virgo loves sex, so the chemistry between Virgo and Scorpio is perceptible. Virgo is enchanted by Scorpio's sensuality, and Scorpio in turn is seduced by Virgo's unassuming attractiveness.

They both automatically know how to satisfy each other's lustful desires. However, outside the bedroom, this couple must work hard to maintain their relationship.

Virgo and Sagittarius *are the most entertaining signs of the zodiac. Virgo's humor is based on tonalities, while Sagittarius' energy creates legends. When they pair up, they make a festive duo. But beyond Sagittarius' recreation, this couple must strive to ensure a healthy relationship.*

When Virgo's thoroughness takes a turn for the worse, it can become fussy, which is confusing to the bohemian Sagittarius, who believes that small details are less important than the big picture.

For this relationship to work, Sagittarius must feel pity for Virgo's irritation, and Virgo must be ready to accept Sagittarius' turbulent inclinations. If they can do this together, they will be sure to enjoy a very entertaining relationship.

Virgo and Capricorn *are a match made in heaven, both are earth signs, calculating, enterprising and sensible. However, because this relationship is so cautious, both partners will have to be vigilant to avoid being too methodical.*

The Capricorn bossy Capricorn may start treating Virgo like a slave, which may make Virgo feel resentful. This couple should infuse energy into their relationship through spontaneous adventures. If the relationship is not too pleasurable, this relationship is meant to last.

Virgo and Aquarius *are very knowledgeable about their realities. These methodical signs admire exploring methods, nuancing their environment with subtle reflections and diligently outlined points of view.*

However, despite their reciprocal love for research, Virgo and Aquarius behaviors are different.

The concrete Virgo is pragmatic and pays a lot of attention to the palpable nuances and details. Aquarius, on the other hand, thinks about things on a general level, so there will be some tension between these signs. But if they can combine their facets, they will form a global vision of the world and as a couple, they have incredible potential.

Virgo and Pisces *are opposite signs that love to be helpful in different ways. Virgo helps pragmatically, while Pisces is more abstract when doing so. Consequently, Virgo and Pisces are pious people who relate on an empathetic level. Virgo's sound mind also helps the erratic Pisces to achieve his purposes, while Pisces' creative acuity encourages Virgo to explore artistic forms of individual expression.*

It is important for each sign to maintain its original identity, and this relationship will subtract the best of each sign and, in doing so, create a radiant union.

Virgo and its Vocation

Virgo is a very thoughtful sign; they do what they must do without drama. They are logical and organized, do not like to draw attention to themselves and can make people around them feel comfortable.

Virgo takes care, and creates a safe environment in the workplace, is very honest, helpful, and expressive.

You can see them providing community service as they are always ready to help.

Best Professions

Virgos are perfectionists, and meticulous when it comes to executing a plan. They are hardworking and helpful. Investigations, detectives, police officers.

Signs not to do business with

Aquarius, Libra, and Sagittarius are signs that make Virgo feel instability. They are totally incompatible for business and investments.

Signs to be associated with

Capricorn, Aquarius, and Taurus. These signs open the way for Virgo. They are very structured and know how to spot a good deal.

Money Rituals

Business Ownership Spell.

You need:

- 1 orange (fruit)

- 3 sheets of green paper

- Olive oil

- Brown sugar

- 1 ceramic plate

- 1 key

- 7 coins of use

- 2 wooden crosses (tied with green ribbon)

- 7 incense

- 7 white rose petals

- 1 red and yellow combination candle

- Herbs: rue, basil, sandalwood, lavender, orange peel and laurel.

- 1 red and white combination candle

- 1 yellow candle

- 1 pyrite stone

- 1 key candle

You must make a hole in the orange so that a candle fits. Write on one of the green papers the name of the person who oversees the property or business contract.

With this paper you are going to surround the base of the yellow candle and place it in the hole you made in the orange candle, then surround it with the seven incense sticks.

You light the candle and while sprinkling it with oil and sugar you repeat in your mind: "Under the powers that I have I demand that (name of the person) only do business with me, that all bad intentions stay away from me".

When the candle is consumed, place it and the orange in a bag and throw them as far away from your house as possible. Do not return the same way.

The next day at night you place on the plate the key, the herbs (rue, basil, sandalwood, lavender, orange peel and laurel), the seven coins, the two crosses, the flower petals, the pyrite, and another green paper with your order.

To the right of the plate, you put the red and yellow candle, and next to it the second green paper in which you will write the address of the house or business. To the left the red and white candle.

You light the candles and repeat under your breath what you wish to be fulfilled.

This ritual should be repeated three days in a row, using the same ceramic plate.

After these days you take from the tray a coin, the pyrite, some of the herbs, the key and one of the crosses, put them in a red bag, which you will keep as an amulet.

The rest of the ingredients are left in the pan, and you add sugar.

On the eighth day you light the key candle and place the last green paper with your wish next to it.

When the candle is consumed, place the remains in a white paper and throw them in a place where there are rocks and that is of four corners.

Protective Money Spell.

You need a small knob with a lid, red ribbon, honey, and three dimes.

Put the honey in the jar and the three coins, close the jar and tie the red ribbon with seven knots.

Place it in the prosperity corner of your home.

Ritual so that Money will always be Present.

You need a white glass bottle, black beans, red beans, sunflower seeds, corn kernels, wheat kernels and a myrrh incense.

You put everything in the bottle in the same order, close it with a cork stopper and pour the smoke from the incense into the bottle.

Then you place it as a decoration in your kitchen.

Gypsy Spell for Prosperity

.

Get a medium-sized clay pot and paint it green. In the bottom put some myrrh, a coin, and a few drops of olive oil. Cover it with a layer of soil and place seeds of your favorite plant.

You add cinnamon and more soil.

You should have it in the dining room of your house and water it so that it grows.

Magic Fumigation for the Economy

You must light three coals in a metal or clay container and add a spoonful of cinnamon, rosemary, and dried apple peels.

You pass it around the house walking clockwise.

Then place white rose petals in a bucket of water and let it stand for three hours.

With this water you will clean your home.

Miracle Essence to Attract Work.

In a dark glass bottle place 32 drops of alcohol, 20 drops of rose water, 10 drops of lavender water and some jasmine leaves. Shake it several times thinking about what you want to attract. You put it in a diffuser, you can use it for your home, business or as a personal perfume.

Spell for Hands and Attract Money.

You need a small clay pot, honey, and Full Moon water. Wash your hands with this liquid but keep the water inside the pot.

Then leave the pot in front of a prosperous business or gambling casino.

Amulet to continue being a Millionaire.

Place under the mattress of your bed a gold coin rolled up with a high denomination bill in a triangle, then tie a golden ribbon and pour two drops of eucalyptus essence on it.

Spell for your Partner to give you Money.

- 2 red roses

- 1 silver coin

- 5 drops of patchouli essence

- 1 pinch of gold dust

- 2 pinches of silver powder

- 1 new portfolio

- 1 gold candle

Place the silver coin inside the wallet, sprinkle the gold and silver powders on it. Light the candle and place it next to the purse with the red roses. You put the patchouli essence on the candle. When the candle burns out, you pick up the remains together with the roses and throw them into the river. Keep the wallet in a place where no one will see it.

Spell to Attract Customers and Sales.

You need:

- 1 glass cup

- 7 drops of sandalwood

- 1 new dropper

- Rainwater

- 1 red carnation

You must fill three quarters of the glass with water. Add the drops of sandalwood and with your hands crush the stem of the carnation. Place the flower inside. Place the cup and these ingredients in a high place somewhere in your business.

Powerful Recipe to Attract Money.

On a Thursday at the hour of Jupiter you should pour into a glass bottle honey, a teaspoon of gold dust, Florida water, a magnet stone, and a white quartz.

Let it rest for three days, then before taking a bath, spread this mixture on your chest, hands, abdomen and soles of your feet, and repeat in your mind: "All my money problems are over today and with the help of the universe I attract abundance, so it is and so it was".

Rinse after you have the mixture on the indicated parts of your body.

If you want to increase your prosperity you can repeat it every Thursday or Sunday. The magnet and the pyrite should be placed in your wallet as lucky charms.

Formula for Prosperity.

You need:

- 1 large candle (should last 7 days)

- Gold dust

- Coffee powder

- Coarse sea salt

- Powdered milk

- Brown sugar

- 1 pencil

- 1 sewing needle

You are going to draw with the needle on the top of the candle a five-pointed star, with the pencil you make a hole in each point of the peaks.

To the five holes you are going to add a pinch of all the ingredients.

You will dedicate this candle to Oshun, the goddess of love and money. You light the candle and let it burn. The remains of the candle should be taken to the river or the sea.

Gleanings of Wheat for Material Prosperity.

You need:

- 3 ears of wheat

- 1 gold spray (of the kind used in ornamentation)

- Sandalwood lotion

You must wet the spikes with the sandalwood cologne. Then you will dye them with the golden spray and place them as follows: one in your pantry, the second one on the refrigerator and the last one as an ornament in any part of your business. When you notice them withered or dirty, throw them away in the trash, wrapped in plastic. Never burn them because you attract bad energies.

Prosperity Ownership Spell

In a large glass of wine and transparent you will pour Full Moon water, then you will introduce a $100 bill and parsley. Every 5 days you will change the water and the parsley if it is withered. If you decide to spend the bill it must be on food, otherwise you will attract poverty.

Spell for Economic Abundance.

When you go to the beach take seven coins of any denomination, stand on the shore, and throw them into the sea asking Yemayá the owner of the seas and the riches hidden in it, to give you fortune and abundance. When you leave, do not look back.

Magic for Prosperity.

You need:

- 1 new golden Buddha

- 1 large red apple

- 1 slice of bread

- 1 bottle of red wine

- 1 pack of incense

- 1 golden plate

Place the Buddha at the entrance of your business or home on top of the golden plate. When you receive visitors ask them to deposit coins or money on the Buddha's plate. Every first day of the month you will place the bottle of wine, the bread, and the apple on the Buddha. You will light an incense and it should remain like this for the whole month. With the money collected, on the first of each month buy the apple, bread, incense, and wine.

Spell to Increase Sales.

You need:

- 1 egg

- 1 small red paint little bottle

- 1 brush

Paint the egg red with the brush, bury it, if possible, on a full moon night.

When you are burying it mentalize all your projects and desires of abundance.

Every month when the full moon returns, change it for a new one painted red and throw the old one in a forest or a river.

Best Countries and Cities to Live In

Countries: *Turkey, Switzerland, Iraq, Kurdistan, Croatia, Greece, Uruguay, and Brazil.*

Countries: Antilles, Crete, Corinth, Athens, Thessaly, Silesia, Baghdad, Paris, Lyon, Toulouse, Heidelberg, Norwich, Boston, Virginia, Madison, Strasbourg, Caracas, Brindisi.

Incense and Essential Oils for Money

Incense and Vanilla Essential Oil. Perfect to enhance prosperity.

Plants for Money

Aloe Vera: *this plant is used in numerous rituals to counteract envy, aloe vera attracts good luck and prosperity in the houses where it is found.*

Quartz for Money

Amethyst Quartz: *A Quartz with many positive energies, it can help you to get a job. You should always have it close to bring you economic prosperity, and help you achieve your goals.*

Money Charms

The Pentacles of Jupiter that will guarantee you Prosperity.

Pentacles are magical figures, capable of transmitting positive energies to their environment. The action of Jupiter's pentacles derives from the combination of letters, signs, and beneficial formulas, they symbolize graphically and mystically a wish. They clearly act on the psyche of people who have visual contact with him.

The largest compilation of pentacles is found in The Clavicles of King Solomon, a volume of high magic attributed to this biblical king. In it are 36 pentacles that have various purposes and among them are the seven pentacles of Jupiter.

Pentacles to Prosper.

The purpose of these pentacles is to provide abundance, to resolve work-related conflicts and to assist in perceiving more directly all kinds of benefits that grant greater prosperity.

Jupiter, the so-called Great Benefic in astrology, is a planet that is related to expansion, optimism, links with powerful people and the ability to make fortune.

You should draw them with great concentration and with the intention that they manifest your will.

The most suitable material is a piece of parchment. Once finished, they should be hung somewhere that is visible such as the cash register or in your wallet (you can print them out).

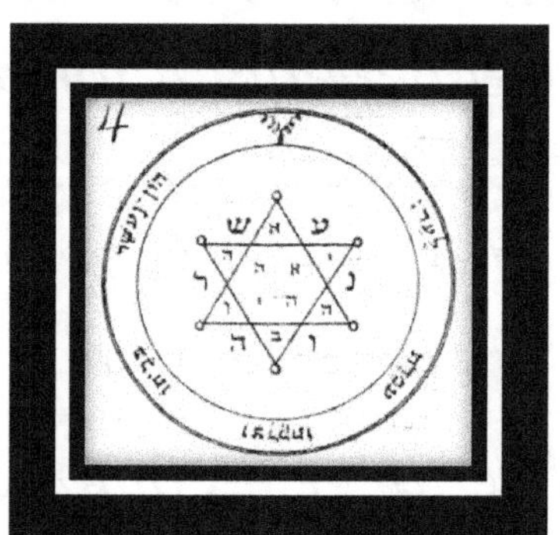

Affirmations to Receive Money

You should perform these decrees for 21 days so that you can see the results, if possible three times a day. If you repeat them out loud, they will be more powerful.

I have the power to create my own world. My dreams materialize because I persevere in them. Everything I set my mind to; I achieve.

I decide today to have an abundant life, with success, love, and happiness. I decide to have all the best, no matter how great. I think of success and abundance.

My magnetic vibration attracts well-being to my life and everything around me. I believe in the power of attraction.

Vacations

Vacations provide physical and mental benefits. It has been proven that vacationing lowers stress levels and benefits the immune system. Sometimes planning a vacation causes stress because there are infinite options and deciding becomes a chimerical task.

Using astrology, understanding your personality provides insight into the ideal vacation spot for you.

__Aries,__ an all-inclusive resort with outdoor sports activities in a warm location such as Punta Cana, Cancun and the Turks and Caicos Islands would be ideal. Australia is an exciting country that offers a wealth of emotions to make your heart race.

__Taurus__, a stay in a luxurious resort on Cayman Island, or a luxurious vacation in Dubai, in a hotel that has all the amenities will be very appealing. Italy is a perfect country because there you will find everything you have always dreamed of love, charm, luxury, wonderful food, and first-class wines.

__Gemini__ loves to feel intellectually engaged. Travel with guided excursions such as a safari in Africa or researching the species of the Galapagos Islands offer the zodiac communicator a luxurious experience.

Cancer, *short trips, surrounded by family and friends. Disney World, enjoying the attractions and its diverse foods is one option. In Orlando, Florida, there are multiple fantastic hotels and resorts, each with a unique and fascinating theme.*

Leo, *staying in a bungalow over the sea in Tahiti is fantastic for this sign. Another luxury alternative, something the lion loves, would be to rent a private tropical island in the Maldives, Fiji, or the Virgin Islands.*

Virgo, *Italy is your best option. This country will keep you well occupied. As an earth sign you connect with the world around you, places like La Romana in the Dominican Republic, Puerto Viejo in Costa Rica, and Belo Horizonte in Brazil will inject life into you.*

Libra, *go for cities with museums. Tropical vacations will not be as satisfying for Libra as touring the Louvre in Paris, the Acropolis Museum in Athens, Greece, the Prado Museum in Madrid, Spain or the Uffizi Gallery in Florence, Italy.*

Scorpion, *spend a few days on a secluded beach with liquor and massages. In Greece, Bali, St. Martin, or Hawaii you will find all these luxuries. Visiting heritage sites near your luxury hotel would be an extraordinary combination of tropical and cultural vacation. Mykonos and Roda in Greece are perfect destinations.*

Sagittarius, *explore the Camino de Santiago, a network of very different paths, all leading to the city of Santiago de Compostela. Each path has its history, heritage, and magic. Sagittarius is a traveler who craves new experiences so in Ireland you will find everything you are looking for.*

Capricorn, *a goal-oriented sign. Vacations where you can make new business relationships. China would be spectacular. Capricorn has a sense of historical value that other signs do not have, so countries like Israel and Egypt where history is present will make you feel at home.*

Aquarius *loves new ideas, unknown places, and new relationships. A fantastic country to visit would be Japan not only for its fascinating history and culture,* *but because each of its regions has something different to offer.*

__Pisces__, a water sign that is happy with tropical vacations. A beachfront hotel would be ideal. The island "La Dique" in the Republic of Seychelles, perhaps the most beautiful beach in the world will be a sure success. Pisces, possessing a calm outlook on life, being ruled by Neptune makes you a creative thinker. Sweden is a country he should visit because there he will find a culture as innovative as he is.

Who is your soul mate according to your zodiac sign?

When we hear the term "soul mates," we usually think of them as referring to members of a couple, i.e., someone with whom you have a strong sentimental-sexual connection. However, legitimate soul mates do not always relate to each other from that point of view, and often are not even interested in the sexual aspect of a relationship.

Your soul mate may not only be your partner, but also your parent, friend, child, grandparent, boss, or sister.

From an astrological point of view and considering that the lessons we need to learn before reaching the next spiritual level are the ones that define the type of affective relationships, we need to develop in life today, we can say that Cancer and Pisces are soul mates of Aries.

With Cancer and Pisces, Aries can not only focus better and resolve conflicts without violence, but also develop empathy, that is, the ability to put themselves in the other's place and learn to share.

These two signs do not like conflicts, and if they do arise, they prefer dialogue to any episode of brutality.

Aries can teach Cancer and Pisces not to need the approval of others, to be more risk-taking, and not to try to please everyone, i.e., to be more assertive.

The sensual Taurus, enemy of change, inbred relative of inertia, has as his soul mate Sagittarius and Gemini, two signs that know that life is a fascinating journey, but not a static one.

They can teach Taurus that it does not have to stay where it no longer must be for fear of uncertainty, and that there will always be certain situations or circumstances that will happen without us expecting them, and without us possessing any power to modify them. Taurus also has a lot to teach these signs.

Lessons of willpower, to have commitments with others, to be committed to what they do and to continue to the end with persistence, without haste or slowness. To have principles, and to be prudent.

Leo can balance a lot of karma with their soul mates belonging to Libra and Aquarius.

A Leo may become obstinate with a wrong idea or belief out of vanity; Libra and Aquarius know that behind an egocentric person there is a low self-esteem.

Libra will teach Leo equanimity and tolerance, to use reasoning and diplomacy to maintain smooth communication. Aquarius, the opposite sign to Leo, equipped with objective and fair judgment as they are never swayed by prejudice, will teach Leo to see people's hearts, to offer their shoulder and give sympathetic words in times of need.

Leo never hesitates when making decisions, and if they do, they do not manifest it, something that Libra should practice.

Fidelity is a hallmark in Leo, something unknown to Aquarius, and the little lions can give him moral lessons.

Virgo, known as perfectionists because of their immense fear of failure, has Scorpio and Capricorn as soul mates. Virgo likes to be rigorous in their decisions and has a prototype in almost every aspect of their life. This selectivity holds them back from following the movement of life.

Virgo will literally tear an entire project apart if they feel it wasn't perfect in the first place, something a Capricorn would never do as their vision will allow them to see that alternative measures can always be taken, without having to start over.

Capricorn is a sign sure of their own space, they don't make meaningless decisions, something Virgo sometimes does.

On the other hand, Scorpio can mitigate the worst and enhance the best of Virgo. Scorpio and Virgo have a practical approach to life; however, Scorpio is much more of a life-lover than Virgo. Scorpio will bring the decisiveness that Virgo lacks, and Virgo will bring control and rationality to the passionate Scorpio.

Virgo will make Capricorn more pleasant and playful at his side, isolating him from that excessive seriousness that he often shows in his face.

The madness

Madness has been revealed throughout history as an obscure, enigmatic, and conflicting truth. It has frightened us, we have ignored it and even accepted it, and as a result, the people who have supposedly suffered from it have been rejected, eliminated, and honored.

Any behavior that is incongruent with our reasoning is not necessarily an act of insanity, but a different way of proceeding.

It is a mistake if, when we feel affected or annoyed by the actions or follies of others, we banish them, since this does not make us more reasonable, balanced, or perfect, but rather makes us just as crazy.

Defining insanity is as complex as defining sanity, but all zodiac signs have their degree of insanity.

Cancer: They are temperamental. This causes them to have an incomprehensible personality seen from the outside. The popularity of crazy people was earned by their inconsistent character that sometimes disturbs the people around them.

Scorpio: They need change to be happy, they can do crazy things just to generate some action. For them having an outburst is normal because they are addicted to change and frenzies.

Pisces*: It is impossible for them not to infect you with their madness. Their instability and imbalance bother the people around them. They see everything as rosy, which makes them be called crazy because they are always floating on a cloud.*

Gemini*: He is famous for his duality. They are sometimes in conflict with themselves. They love challenges that involve danger. They love to plan impromptu adventures and are always ready to border the limits of maximum madness.*

Leo*: When the fire settles in their head, they think that everything that surrounds their life is more urgent than anything else. They are extravagant and have attitudes that for others are considered crazy. They can do things that a reasonable person would never do.*

Aries*: They upset themselves and anyone around them. They are stubborn and like to be the first in everything, even if for that they must commit crazy* *things. They do not know how to take it back, something that leads them to perform irrational acts.*

Aquarius*: A rebellious and free sign, which does not care in the least about the opinion they have of them. They act in a capricious way, with crazy attitudes that break the paradigms.*

Sagittarius: *He is fun, but violent with his desire for action. They do not know how to measure the consequences of their actions, something that many consider madness. It is not strange to see them totally unbridled, crossing the terrain of irresponsibility.*

Libra*: They long for happiness and harmony, and to get it they are willing to do anything crazy. They are unstable, and that leads them to break their commitments, something that many consider crazy.*

Virgo: *They go to extremes and become obsessive. They have a vision of what they want written in stone, no one can give them advice, they do not let themselves be guided. When they do not listen, they commit various follies.*

Taurus: *When an idea lands in their mind there is no one to banish it, even committing crazy things to corroborate their hypothesis. Try to test their patience and you will discover how far their level of madness goes.*

Capricorn: He *forgets absolutely nothing, does not forgive and much less, forgets, if you do something wrong, do not worry because he will remind you for a lifetime to drive you completely crazy. Capricorn is insanely obsessive about control.*

The psychology behind the lottery.

Lottery games are very popular all over the world.

We all have the impossible dream of winning the lottery, since the illusion of being millionaires, by a stroke of luck, even if the odds are minimal, is the main reason why people play.

Players perceive that the cost of the lottery ticket, in relation to the profits they would obtain if they won, is miniscule. We always perceive risk emotionally, and if it causes us pleasure, we tend to see the risk as insignificant and neutralize the emotion of danger, focusing only on the benefits.

Players see the lottery as a unique opportunity to be rewarded by investing little money, and with little exposure to risk.

Games have both traditional and superstitious aspects. Some people always play the same numbers because they are their favorites, relate them to a significant date, or have dreamed them.

Others play at a specific time, day, or place. When we think we are in control, we feel confident, because when we choose the numbers ourselves, instead of playing at random, although the chances of being right are the same, we have the impression that we are controlling destiny, and that the chances are in our favor.

There are people who only play for fun, in these cases the lottery transcends the economic cost, becoming a fun that is enlivened when they conjecture everything, they can do with the money they would acquire.

There are five psychological descriptions of individual lottery players:

The adventurer, *who is bewitched by games involving large sums of money, speculating with random numbers, and with planned numbers.*

The competitor, *who insists on showing off through gambling that he bets to win.*

The greedy, *who has no boundaries for gambling, and is not afraid to take risks when betting.*

The tactician, *never playing risky, looks for tactics, strategies, and numerical sets when playing the numbers.*

The superstitious person, *who always plays the same number combinations, uses talismans, rituals, or will buy his tickets on a specific date and place.*

Is there a trick or formula to win the lottery?

That question is still unanswered. There are many who speculate, and claim, that you are more likely to be struck by lightning before you win the lottery. Although others study the odds with great perseverance and subtlety.

Playing the lottery, or any other game of chance if it is done with measure, is a cheap way to buy illusions and confidence in the future. The complication arises when the person does not control his impulses to play, generating an addiction to gambling and falling into compulsive gambling.

A gambling addict is an individual to whom gambling causes great difficulties at work and in his family relationships, since losses induce him to gamble larger amounts of money with the aspiration of recovering the lost money. This becomes a vicious circle, and the only way to solve it is with psychotherapeutic treatment.

The best gifts for zodiac signs

Gift giving is a universal way to show that we care and appreciate a person, but gift buying can be a challenge, for some a real headache.

The planets can help you once, knowing the zodiac sign of the person, you may be able to make the ideal gift.

*Fire signs: **Aries, Leo and Sagittarius** like gifts that make them feel important, related to sports, travel, and technology.*

A professional digital camera, the latest model of iPhone, a plane ticket with hotel included to an exotic tourist spot or with historical background, business books, sportswear or exercise equipment, lottery tickets, bottles of fine wine and exclusive branded shoes will please these signs greatly.

***Taurus, Virgo and Capricorn**, who belong to the earth element, are sometimes traditional, but that doesn't mean they don't like gifts from recognized brands.*

A painting of a famous painter, a belt or briefcase to carry their work papers, a wallet with their initials, branded perfumes, massages or body treatments, a pet, bathrobes, cozy pajamas, or even aromatherapy diffusers will make them happy.

*Air signs: **Gemini, Libra and Aquarius** are not materialistic, and the functionality of a gift is much more important than the price. Their imagination is abundant, and anything that stimulates this capacity appeals to them.*

A cell phone, computer or IPad, books on personal growth, spirituality, philosophy and alternative therapies, self-help and economic empowerment courses, a telescope, tickets to the opera or theater, an animal that does not have to be caged, quartz, essential oils, incense, and after-bath colognes will be highly appreciated by these signs.

***Cancer, Scorpio and Pisces**, the water signs, will love personalized gifts. Cooking utensils, a romantic dinner on the beach under the moonlight, a relaxing massage in a spa, daring lingerie, slippers or a comfortable sofa to watch TV, a bottle of champagne, scented candles, amulets, astrology books, a set of tarot cards, lotions, perfumes and beauty accessories, wine, cookies, preserves and all variety of gourmet products are on the list of gifts that these signs will accept with great pleasure.*

Giving gifts is a blessing, it is a gesture of generosity; giving gifts is a symbolic act that represents a compliment, an attention to someone we want to please and symbolizes the affection we profess.

When we give gifts, relationships are improved and strengthened, and joy is generated.

The zodiac signs and their fears.

The twelve signs of the zodiac symbolize twelve essential archetypes of the human personality, but at the same time they are psychological prototypes, which is why each of the zodiac signs has a very specific and personal fear.

Let us remember that fear is an essential human alarm and defense mechanism. It only becomes a problem when it is excessive.

*Fears are insecurities and sometimes we project them with the opposite actions as is the case of the **Aries** sign; recognized for their iron will, nothing and nobody paralyzes them. They love to control everything, and their most ingrained fear is to fail or ask for help, because for them this is synonymous of weakness.*

***Taurus** is the most stubborn of the earth signs. Change terrifies them, as well as running out of money, they spend their lives saving because poverty frightens them.*

***Gemini**, the communicator of the zodiac, a bit anxious and insecure, they try to attract attention because they dread looking boring. Legitimate children of the*

Moon, Cancers love their safety zone because no one can hurt them there, they are terrified of loneliness and rejection.

***Leo**, the king of the zodiac, leaders and brave, were not born to lose. Their most ingrained fear is to go unnoticed; they prefer to be spoken ill of, but not to be ignored.*

*The master of neatness **Virgo** sometimes becomes compulsive with the subject of health, so they are hypochondriacs. Their main fear is getting sick, but disorganization scares them more than anything else.*

*Exceptionally intelligent **Librans** are indecisive and therein lies their primary fear: making decisions. Another of their fears is loneliness.*

*Enigmatic and seductive **Scorpios** have an elephant's memory, they fear betrayal and if you do something they dislike, they will keep it from you forever. Never keep a secret from a Scorpio.*

*The adventurer of the zodiac, **Sagittarius is** terrified of commitment because the demands are terrifying. They* *are very funny, but behind that smile hides the fear of being deceived.*

*Demanding to the extreme, **Capricorns** never stray from their goals; their main fear is to make mistakes, especially at the professional level. They are self-sacrificing and fear not achieving their dreams.*

*The rebellious and utopian **Aquarius** fear losing their freedom, this would mean losing their own essence. They always have many friendships, but none of them bind them. They need the group, but do not want the group to need them.*

*Peace is synonymous with **Pisces**, they hate confrontations. Compassionate to the core, they are afraid to see others suffer. They are a little insecure, have stage fright and fear rejection.*

Some old astrology books hold Saturn totally responsible for fear in a natal chart, I think that for fear to originate, the alliance of several planets with their corresponding energies must manifest.

That is, fears are represented by several planets linked by aspects, there is no specific planet that is necessarily related to the development of any type of fear.

Moon in Virgo

Virgo is motivated by perfectionism and being useful to others. Virgo's talent lies in analysis.

The Moon in Virgo tends to experience emotions in a secure and stable way.

The lesson of the Moon in Virgo is to learn to move beyond the physical and connect with the spiritual, i.e., you must learn to broaden your perspectives.

If your Moon is in Virgo, you are always looking for ways to improve the environment around you, and you are on the lookout for any imperfections that need to be fixed. You like to care for and serve others, and you do this through small favors. You like to make a difference in any aspect of your life.

Virgo is a sign that is always busy with details and struggles with the little things. It is excellent at picking up on small emotional changes and has an excellent sense of boundaries.

One of the most important lessons for the person with Moon in Virgo is to accept that perfection does not exist. This Moon very easily loses its sense of perspective and feels threatened when it discovers imperfections that it is unable to fix. When this happens, your instinctive reaction is to be critical. Your ego thinks that if you exaggerate something that needs to be fixed someone else will fix it. Your need for security is based on details, but you only care about the things you think you can influence. If you happen to find yourself in a situation that is out of your control, you don't worry about it no matter how many flaws you find. That is, you are aware of how much you can influence, and what you can fix.

When the Moon in Virgo feels threatened, you begin to focus on small, unimportant details. In short, if you don't have the ability to fix something that you feel needs fixing, you will focus on something that you can fix.

The importance of the Ascendant Sign

The sun sign has a major impact on who we are, but the ascendant is what really defines us, and that could even be the reason why you don't identify with some traits of your zodiac sign.

Really the energy that your sun sign gives you makes you feel different from the rest of the people, for that reason, when you read your horoscope sometimes you feel identified and gives sense to some predictions, and that happens because it helps you to understand how you could feel and what will happen to you, but it only shows you a percentage of what could really be.

The ascendant on the other hand differs from the sun sign because it reflects who we are superficially, that is, how others see you or the energy you transmit to people, and this is so real that it may be the case that you meet someone and if you predict their sign you may have discovered their ascendant sign and not their sun sign.

In summary, the characteristics you see in someone when you first meet them is the Ascendant, but since our lives are affected by the way we relate to others, the Ascendant has a major impact on our daily lives.

It is a bit complex to explain how the rising sign is calculated or determined, because it is not the position of a planet that determines it, but the sign that was rising on the eastern horizon at the time of your birth, as opposed to your sun sign, which depends on the precise time you were born.

Thanks to technology and the Universe today is easier than ever to know this information, of course if you know your birth time, or if you have an idea of the time but there is not a margin of more than hours, because there are many websites that make the calculation by entering the data, astro.com is one of them, but there is infinite.

This way, when you read your horoscope you can also read your ascendant and know more personalized details, you will see that from now on if you do this your way of reading the horoscope will change and you will know why that Sagittarius is so modest and pessimistic if in fact they are so exaggerated and optimistic, and this is perhaps because he has a Capricorn Ascendant, or because that Scorpio colleague is always talking about everything, no doubt he has a Gemini Ascendant.

I am going to synthesize the characteristics of the different Ascendants, but this is also very general since these characteristics are modified by planets in conjunction with the Ascendant, planets aspecting the Ascendant, and the position of the sign's ruling planet on the Ascendant.

For example, a person with an Aries Ascendant with its ruling planet, Mars, in Sagittarius will respond to the environment a little differently than another person, also with an Aries Ascendant, but whose Mars is in Scorpio.

Similarly, a person with a Pisces Ascendant who has Saturn conjunct him will "behave" differently than someone with a Pisces Ascendant who does not have that aspect.

All these factors modify the Ascendant, astrology is very complex, and horoscopes are not read or made with tarot cards, because astrology is not only an art but also a science.

It can be common to confuse these two practices, and this is because, although they are two totally different concepts, they have some points in common. One of these common points is based on their origin and is that both procedures have been known since ancient times.

They are also similar in the symbols they use, since both present ambiguous symbols that need to be interpreted, requiring specialized reading and training to know how to interpret these symbols.

There are thousands of differences, but one of the main ones is that while in tarot the symbols are perfectly understandable at first glance, being figurative cards, although it is necessary to know how to interpret them well, in astrology we observe an abstract system which is necessary to know previously to interpret them, and of course it must be said that, although we can recognize the tarot cards, anyone can not interpret them correctly.

Interpretation is also a difference between the two disciplines because while tarot does not have an exact time reference, since the cards are placed in time only thanks to the questions asked in the corresponding spread, astrology does refer to a specific position of the planets in history, and the interpretation systems used by both are diametrically opposed.

The astrological chart is the basis of astrology, and the most important aspect to make the prediction. The astrological chart must be perfectly elaborated for the reading to be successful and to learn more about the person.

To draw up a birth chart, it is necessary to know all the data about the birth of the person in question.

It must be known exactly, from the exact time it was delivered, to the place where it was done.

The position of the planets at the time of birth will reveal to the astrologer the points he needs to draw up the birth chart.

Astrology is not only about knowing your future, but also about knowing the important points of your existence, both present and past, to make better decisions to decide your future.

Astrology will help you to know yourself better, so that you can change the things that block you or enhance your qualities.

And if the astrological chart is the basis of astrology, the tarot reading is fundamental in the latter discipline. Like who makes you the astrological chart, the seer who makes you the tarot spread, will be the key to the success of your reading, so it is best to ask for tarot readers recommended, and although surely you cannot answer specifically to all the questions you ask yourself in your life, a correct reading of the tarot spread, and the cards that come out in the roll, will help guide you about the decisions you make in your life.

In summary, astrology, and tarot use symbolism, but the main question is how all this symbolism is interpreted.

truly a person who masters both techniques will undoubtedly be a great help to the people who will ask for advice.

Many astrologers combine both disciplines, and regular practice has taught me that both usually flow very well, providing an enriching component in all prediction issues, but they are not the same and you cannot do a horoscope with tarot cards, nor can you do a tarot reading with an astrological chart.

Ascendant in Virgo

People with Ascendants in Virgo are concerned about their health and lifestyle. Many people with this Ascendant direct their attention to the physical body. This Ascendant should remember that perfection is found in balance.

In the sentimental area, the Ascendant Virgo, if they are in a relationship, should try to get rid of the bad thoughts that derive from the fact that their partner is not "perfect" or does not share their vision of order.

Individuals with Ascendants in Virgo must learn to be more flexible and to manage imperfection to lead a healthier life in tune with the universe.

Aries - Virgo Ascendant

This combination of signs is contradictory, because of the prudence of Virgo and the impatience and recklessness of Aries. Professionally, these people are respected by their colleagues thanks to their cordial manner. They usually excel in jobs that require a certain technique, although this does not prevent them from being successful in any type of work thanks to their endurance and perseverance. They are also hard workers.

In love, they are demanding and capable of seeing the defects of others from a hundred miles away, even causing them problems because they do not know how to keep quiet about what they think. It is not very easy for them to get easily involved in a relationship.

Virgo Ascendant with Aries are prone to become workaholics, do not know how to relax, and take on more than they can handle.

Taurus - Virgo Ascendant

Taurus with Virgo Ascendant are rational, practical, and demanding with themselves.

At work they tend to concentrate on anything that involves mental work. They like to work on ambitious projects and study how to make them successful.

In their love relationships, they are people who behave elegantly and affectionately. The only thing is that they will not show this facet until they feel confident.

They can become arrogant people, boasting of their knowledge, although they do not really possess it. They are also skeptical of any kind of belief.

Gemini - Virgo Ascendant

Gemini Ascendant Virgo are people with a variety of contrasts and who stand out for their particularity. It is a combination that challenges itself, as it seeks practicality in everything, but also the most abstract part.

They are not ambitious at work, but with Virgo's attention to detail and Gemini's mental agility, it is not difficult for them to achieve the goals they set for themselves.

In relationships they spend a lot of work with their emotions, becoming extremely demanding people and that makes it difficult for them to be with someone and commit.

Cancer - Virgo Ascendant

People of the sign Cancer with Virgo Ascendant are very careful and protective of their family and close friends. They care immensely for their safety and well-being and know how to maintain a friendship.

At work they are very organized and empathetic, something that helps them to keep the people they interact with happy.

In love they are people who have difficulty initiating a relationship, as they are very shy. But once they take the step, or find the right person, they are demanding and affectionate with that specific person.

In the emotional sphere there is a negative side, as Virgo's extremism for perfection makes these people channel all their emotional frustrations with those around them.

Leo - Virgo Ascendant

Leo with Virgo Ascendant are people with a refined practical sense, which is beneficial for the daily routine. They are introspective people who value solitude and intimacy.

They are methodical and analytical individuals, but sometimes they are very proud in the professional area.

In their relationships the common expression "a picture says more than a thousand words" applies 100% and they are also extremely demanding with what they want.

They never get emotionally involved until they are convinced that the person is the right one.

Some are very self-critical and proud, which makes it difficult for them to establish fruitful relationships.

Virgo - Virgo Ascendant

This zodiacal combination reinforces all the potentials of the Virgo sign, the good and the bad. They are extremely perfectionist and logical people. They always have their feet on the ground and are not idealistic.

In the professional field, they are hard workers who do not give up on a project until it meets the requirements of perfection that they demand of themselves. They do not like to be helped because they consider that nobody does it better than they do. In other words, they do not know how to delegate, and this can be negative in certain circumstances.

In relationships they are distrustful people and need to be sure of a relationship to become fully involved. That is why most are single for long periods of time.

Obsession with details is his undoing.

Libra - Virgo Ascendant

These people are very practical and helpful to everyone.

In their profession, they are very hard-working and seek to achieve financial independence as soon as possible.

In their sentimental relationships they are committed, honest and faithful people. They are not people who like strong adventures because they prefer a traditional style life.

Some are prone to be greedy and end up financially bankrupt.

Scorpio - Virgo Ascendant

Scorpio with Virgo Ascendant are the people who do not mince words, they say what they feel without filters.

Occasionally this can be beneficial for personal relationships, since unlike the other signs they have no problem expressing what they think, even if they are unpleasant things.

This combination is great for a research job as Scorpio's intuition meets Virgo's love of detail, making these people the best at solving any problem.

At work they are very responsible, they always look for the root of problems and do not rest until they are solved.

In their romantic relationships they are quite closed, but once they open with someone, they are faithful.

The dark side of this astral combination is that they are manipulative people and will try to impose their truth.

Sagittarius - Virgo Ascendant

Sagittarius with Virgo Ascendant prioritizes their family above all else. They stand out for having a great mental capacity which helps them to progress quickly in any profession.

Their work will always be in tune with their family stability. They are emotionally reserved and have many moral concerns. They find it difficult to find a suitable partner, but when they do, they can share all their secrets with them.

The family may abuse these individuals.

Capricorn - Virgo Ascendant

Capricorns with Virgo Ascendant are hard-working people who are constantly developing their skills and finding their vocation during this process.

They are people who prefer to work for themselves, since they cannot stand someone less qualified giving them orders. They have a great ability and capacity to generate money, and if they find their true vocation, they will have no problem in dedicating all the hours that this work requires.

They are selective in their relationships and do not want to waste time with ephemeral or banal relationships.

Sometimes they can become obsessed with work, even going so far as to live to work rather than work to live.

Aquarius - Virgo Ascendant

This astrological combination causes Aquarius' desire for independence and Virgo's need for stability to clash, resulting in an unconventional scenario.

This mix of qualities makes them the perfect employee as they are very organized and methodical people who know how to communicate and come up with original ideas.

In their relationships, they are prone to affairs and do not like commitment. They are very unloving and quite funny people. They possess an exceptional mind and can be very difficult emotionally which makes a relationship difficult.

Pisces - Virgo Ascendant

Pisces Ascendant Virgo are balanced people as they combine the prudence and organization of Virgo with the empathy and sensitivity of Pisces.

At work they excel in their creativity and know how to deal very well with their colleagues and those around them. They can lead groups of people.

For them, being in a relationship is necessary, and when they are committed, they dedicate themselves body and soul to that person.

Sometimes they get carried away by first impressions without really getting to know the person.

Saturn in Pisces, one of the most important astrological events.

March 7, 2023, was one of the most important days in that year's astrological calendar. Saturn, the stern teacher, and lord of karma, clashed with Pisces, the dreamer. This transit of Saturn in Pisces, which will last until February 2026, has not been a welcome mix.

Saturn is a planet of responsibility and strict authority, disciplining and structuring us as it transits through the zodiac. Saturn wants to make sure how we are achieving our goals, and when this planet moves through Pisces, the most spiritual sign, some important proposals are headed our way. Pluto and Saturn, shifting so unison, will bring a gigantic energetic volcano, and guaranteed to be an unforgettable period.

This may sound like a formula for battle, but this energetic combo can be effective and profitable.

Saturn is not satisfied in Pisces. It is difficult for him to found structures and build reality when everything is shifting. Pisces is a dual sign, so it can express itself in opposite ways; it can be both transcendental and practical. There is the possibility that Saturn in Pisces indicates the construction of forms above or below the water, or to dominate the water, such as pipelines, aqueducts, and ports. But it can also reveal the collapse of these structures due to hurricanes or structural fragility.

The Pisces archetype is contradictory to Saturn. It represents utopia, creativity, spirituality, and esotericism, as well as dreams, illusions, lies and escapism. It symbolizes the aspiration to flow like the sea, breaking down boundaries and restrictions.

The last transit of Saturn in Pisces was from May 1993 to April 1996, this stage saw the results of the collapse of the Soviet Union in 1989 which caused aftermath worldwide and crushed the Russian economy. Russia launched the first Chechen war in 1994 which lasted until 1996. The International Criminal Tribunal for the former Yugoslavia was established in The Hague in May 1993 to prosecute war crimes committed during the Yugoslav war in the early 1990s.

On the other hand, the Bosnian war between Croats, Bosnians and Serbs spread with cruelties and ethnic cleansing, and various executions. The war ended in 1995, and most of the Bosnian Serb commanders were convicted of genocide and crimes against humanity. In 1994 the Rwandan genocide began when Hutu gangs murdered more than 700,000 Tutsis, and untold numbers of women were raped during the massacre, which finally ended in July. The Iraq disarmament crisis, after the end of the first Gulf War, was at its height with a lot of noise and no trust among those involved.

A sect in Switzerland called the "Order of the Solar Temple", carried out a chain of crimes and mass suicides, and here in the United States, Timothy McVeigh murdered 168 people in the Oklahoma City bombing. It was during this Saturn transit through Pisces that O.J. Simpson was arrested for the murder of his ex-wife and boyfriend, and released after a lengthy trial that was a Hollywood-style spectacle.

In London, Fred West and his wife Rose were jailed after extractions in their backyard of the bodies of multiple murder victims.

South Africa had its first multiracial elections, and Nelson Mandela was elected president, later abolishing the death penalty in that country. Russia and China signed an agreement to stop provoking each other with their nuclear devices, and the Nuclear Non-Proliferation Treaty was endlessly amplified by 170 countries. In Australia, it was agreed to compensate indigenous people who were evicted during nuclear tests in the 1950s and 1960s.

Other events during the transit of Saturn in Pisces include religious currents, ideological movements such as socialism and leftism, the transmission of diseases and contagions, destructive behaviors induced by panic, an increase in the use of drugs and development of all types of art, as well as the means of maritime transportation.

Saturn in Pisces will see to it that we cannot use spirituality or fear to avoid certain conflicts that we must face. We can meditate, go to spend a hundred years in Tibet, and use the most powerful mantras in the universe, but at some point, we must also act.

During the last few years that Saturn has transited Aquarius, there has been a need to focus on individuality and be more genuine, rather than tolerate coercion from those around us.

Although Aquarius is a sign known for dancing to its own beat, as Saturn is all about limitations, it has pushed us to sit alone with ourselves (remember the restrictions during the pandemic) and look at where we can place ourselves to create healthy boundaries.

All those lessons prepared us for what lies ahead with Saturn in Pisces. We will begin to be more sensible about how to add spirituality into our daily lives, while retaining an understanding of how to structure ourselves. Many people will abandon or question religions or dogmas.

Of course, there are many who will not savor this period, among them are religious guides and those who promote conspiracy theories. We will see conflicts between individuals of dissimilar religions, and many tendencies to try to dominate what others choose to believe.

We need to accept that just because others disagree with our beliefs, it doesn't mean they are wrong. It simply indicates that their views are different, because at the end of the day, Pisces stands for inclusiveness. Something we lack.

As Pisces and Neptune rule the entertainment business, major studios and record companies will close, and many artists who have been connected to those studios will decide to create their own. If you are an artist, it will be in your interest to use your work beneficially, rather than letting the big companies at the top enjoy the dividends.

There will be less interest in special effects and a greater orientation toward self-contained films and themes that reflect the everyday. We will appreciate the beauty around us and be less motivated by glamour.

Karma often tends to be seen as evil, but reaping what you sow is not bad if you have behaved well.

Working with our karmic and subconscious baggage, understanding the past and being ready to let go, is critical to navigate this transit and come out of it successfully. If you dodge this, Saturn will punish you, but if you embrace it, you will arrive at a place that is predestined for something great.

Saturn's placement in our natal chart indicates where we are compelled to gain control of reality and assume greater responsibility.

Pisces is the last sign of the zodiac, so Saturn's movement here also indicates an end or completion point for a much larger cycle.

Pisces is a water sign representing light, darkness, and the invisible worlds. It is known for its abstract ideas, and creativity. Pisces is mutable, which means it is adaptable, and open to the energies of the world around it. Saturn is a very solid energy. It rules over law, responsibilities and restrictions, and its energy can sometimes feel like a wake-up call, bringing us back to reality and making us face the consequences of our actions.

Saturn's presence in Pisces could feel a bit heavy because of all this, as the normally watery, intuitive, and sensitive Piscean energy will be forced to become a bit more reserved.

To understand it better you can think of it this way: if Pisces is smooth flowing water, Saturn's presence will build dams, and these holds can direct the water in a productive and beneficial direction, but it can also feel more oppressive or controlling.

However, there is a way to create a balance between these two energies, as the creative, intangible, and external ideas of the Piscean energy can get some roots thanks to Saturn.

Saturn has a practical energy, so, if we combine this with the creativity of Pisces, there is a balance that can be achieved to help us take our creative ideas and bring them to life or even turn them into a business.

Pisces is also connected to religion and spirituality, so with Saturn there could be many questions around religion and spirituality and how it is connected to the rules that govern society, the spiritual industry may also get a wake-up call under this energy, or on a personal level your own attitudes and beliefs about your spiritual or religious connection will change.

Saturn really wants us to step up and take responsibility for our lives and act in accordance with our authentic selves.

Saturn may impose limits and restrictions that make us feel trapped or suffocated, but this is only so that we can take the time to discover what we really want and what we are willing to stand for.

Another way to get more information about this powerful planetary transit is to think about the themes that developed in your life the last time Saturn was in Pisces, which was from 1994 to 1996, to get additional information about what this cycle can bring you.

How will it affect the Virgo Sign?

Saturn in Pisces will bring revelations when it comes to your relationships. These are not just your romantic relationships, but all the relationships you have with others, how you connect and relate to those around you.

Saturn's energy can manifest as that of a strict teacher, giving you hard lessons and challenges, but this is all in the name of growth and maturity.

Saturn wants us to level up, wants us to unlock our full potential and become masters of our lives. Because Saturn in Pisces is activating your relationships, it could very well be that a real master crosses your path.

This teacher can come in the form of a costume or be a mentor to you. This teacher can be a challenger at work, your partner or someone who seeks support.

This teacher could also come in the form of life lessons. With your relationships under review, you are likely to discover what you want out of life and who you want to surround yourself with. If a relationship has been on dry ground, Saturn in Pisces will bring the stability needed to help you decide.

You may decide that this relationship is no longer for you, or you may get a wake-up call and decide that you want to resolve whatever is going on. Saturn will guide you to the best answer for you.

But first, you may need to do some inner work. How are you going to know what you want from others if you don't know yourself first? Our relationships can be very revealing about who we are and what we want. Sometimes we need to be in a relationship that is not what we want us to realize what we want.

This may be a possible manifestation of Saturn in Pisces. You may also find yourself finally attracting that perfect partner or relationship after years of trial and error.

Saturn wants us to make a commitment, so what do you want to commit to? Who do you want to commit to? These are the kinds of questions Saturn can produce within you. Having Saturn in this placement can also be a positive omen for marriage or forging deeper commitments to those around us.

All you can do here is follow your heart, Saturn often shows us who is worth fighting for, and who is simply dampening our soul and spirit.

Saturn can sometimes bring some irritating energy into our relationships, and this is where we need to set boundaries. Learning to set boundaries with others is another great lesson from Saturn in Pisces for you.

Part of setting good boundaries is also learning to break down some old boundaries that are rooted in fear. You may also find that the fog lifts so that you can see the truth of those you have chosen to surround yourself with. If there has been any deception, Saturn can reveal it so you can move forward with the truth.

These are all things you may be called upon to work on while Saturn transits Pisces. Essentially, by the time Saturn is done with its journey through Pisces, you're going to connect with others on a whole new level. You'll be more secure and more confident when it comes to who you want to keep close to you.

You'll also feel more confident when it comes to the boundaries you need to set with others. This all sounds amazing, and of course, the road to get there may not always feel easy.

Saturn in Pisces is directly opposite you Virgo in the wheel of the zodiac, so you will feel this transit harder than others. Since Saturn is all about rules and laws, its journey through Pisces can cause contractual problems for you. If you are closing any contracts, make sure they are what you want and don't get carried away by the wishes of those around you.

If problems arise for you under this transit, return to responsibility. What do you need to take responsibility for? Addressing that side of things can help you alleviate whatever it is you are disputing.

As the Lord of Karma, Saturn will always make sure that justice is done eventually, you may just have to be a little patient along the way to get there. If you must take some losses, rest assured that something good will prosper from that in time.

Even if things fall apart, Saturn has a way of putting you on the path you are meant to be on.

We all come here with a soul contract, an agreement we conceived before we entered our physical body. Saturn is so closely tied to your soul contract, it knows what it's doing and without revealing too much, it's going to help you get there.

Saturn knows at the soul level what we are here to do, and he is going to guide us to get back on course, or to keep pushing further. If things fade, if relationships break up, if painful truths are unearthed, if we are struggling with contractual issues, it is all just to get back to our true selves.

Saturn in Pisces' unique gift to you is that you will know what you want from the people around you. You will know what and with whom you are willing to compromise.

You will develop a more subtle sense of who you want to keep close to you and how you want to be in your relationships. Relationship work is always one of the most challenging jobs we will do, but your intuitive and practical spirit will guide you through it.

Bibliography

Some information was extracted from the books published by the authors: Love for all Hearts, Money for all Pockets and Horoscope 2022 and 2024.

Articles written in the Nuevo Herald by one of the writers.

About the Authors

In addition to her astrological knowledge, Alina A. Rubi has an abundant professional education; she holds certifications in Psychology, Hypnosis, Reiki, Bioenergetic Crystal Healing, Angelic Healing, Dream Interpretation and is a Spiritual Instructor. Rubi has knowledge of Gemology, which she uses to program stones or minerals and turn them into powerful Amulets or Talismans of protection.

Rubi has a practical and results-oriented character, which has allowed him to have a special and integrating vision of several worlds, facilitating solutions to specific problems.

Alina writes the Monthly Horoscopes for the website of the American Association of Astrologers; you can read them at www.astrologers.com. At this moment she writes a weekly column in the newspaper El Nuevo Herald on spiritual topics, published every Sunday in digital form and on Mondays in print. He also has a program and weekly Horoscope on the YouTube channel of this newspaper. Her Astrological Yearbook is published every year in the newspaper "Diario las Américas", under the column Rubi Astrologa.

Rubi has written several articles on astrology for the monthly publication "Today's Astrologer", has taught classes in Astrology, Tarot, Palm Reading, Crystal Healing, and Esotericism.

She has weekly videos on esoteric topics on her YouTube channel: Rubi Astrologa. She had her own Astrology show broadcasted daily through Flamingo T.V., she has been interviewed by several T.V. and radio programs, and every year she publishes her "Astrological Yearbook" with the horoscope sign by sign, and other interesting mystical topics.

She is the author of the books "Rice and Beans for the Soul" Part I, II, and III, a compilation of esoteric articles, published in English, Spanish, French, Italian and Portuguese. "Money for All Pockets", "Love for All Hearts", "Health for All Bodies", Astrological Yearbook 2021, Horoscope 2022, Rituals and Spells for Success in 2022, Spells and Secrets, Astrology Classes, Rituals and Charms 2024 and Chinese Horoscope 2024 are all available in five languages: English, Italian, French, Japanese and German.

Rubi is fluent in English and Spanish and combines all her talents and knowledge in her readings. She currently resides in Miami, Florida.

For more information you can visit **the website** *www.esoterismomagia.com*

Alina A. Rubi is the daughter of Alina Rubi. She is currently studying psychology at Florida International University.

Since she was a child, she has been interested in all metaphysical and esoteric subjects and has practiced astrology and Kabbalah since she was four years old. She has knowledge of Tarot, Reiki, and Gemology. She is not only the author, but also the editor, together with her sister Angeline A. Rubi, of all the books published by her and her mother.

For more information, please contact her by email: **rubiediciones29@gmail.com**